Learn to Preach
Before Next Weekend

By

James Richard Wibberding

Big Fish Publishing Inc.

Telford, PA 18969

Published by
Big Fish Publishing Inc.
51 West Summit Avenue
Telford, PA 18969

Cover photography
Albert Lacey

Printed in the United States of America
ISBN 0-9777982-1-6

Table of Contents

Preface

The words of James humble me as I write. He warns, "Not many of you should presume to be teachers, my brothers, because you know that we who teach will be judged more strictly" (James 3:1 NIV).

I am keenly aware that others are more qualified to write this book than I am. I write it because no one else has. Thus, it arises from a need. During my years as pastor of various congregations, I have had the opportunity to teach church elders and others to preach but have yet to find a simple *and* complete manual that is written with the amateur in mind.

Despite my lack of stature in the scholarly community, I feel that I have drawn together the best of the field. I stand on the shoulders of many great preachers to offer this simple, complete guide to the basics of preaching. Whether you are a professional in the making or a weekend warrior, I believe this small volume will help you preach with excellence.

James Richard Wibberding

Sermons in a Nutshell

A Lesson On Fear

For weeks, my spine sent out tremors. Why did I ever think I could do this? I knew God didn't make mistakes but a deep suspicion began to set in that this *could* be his first. Of course I didn't believe that but I couldn't see past the clouds either—dark clouds of fear that hung thick over my thoughts whenever that preaching appointment came to mind. It would be my first, *if* I lived through it.

I had fought God's call, not because I didn't want to serve but because I didn't think I could. Perhaps *you* have felt that tug at your own heart. If you have ever longed for revival and wished you could spark it in those around you, it might be God's Spirit urging you to take a risk, to preach. But, risk is scary.

I can still hear my shaky voice sounding in the tight quarters of my college dorm room: "God, I can't preach and I'm too young." I had been feeling his call for weeks. I

Risk is scary.

3

continued, "But, if you are really telling me to do this, you'll have to show me." I then told God, in no uncertain terms, that I was tired of wrestling with the issue and wished to settle it once and for all. I said, "I'm going to open my Bible now. Please help me open to the right text."

What followed was a moment like nothing I had experienced. Yes, I asked God to say just what he meant, and I wished he would, but I didn't expect it. I opened directly to Jeremiah 1 and my eyes fell on verses 4-7:

> *"The word of the LORD came to me, saying, 'Before I formed you in the womb I knew you, before you were born I set you apart; I appointed you as a prophet to the nations.' 'Ah, Sovereign LORD,' I said, 'I do not know how to speak; I am only a child.' But the LORD said to me, 'Do not say, "I am only a child." You must go to everyone I send you to and say whatever I command you.'"*

A chill ran through me, and then a shot of exhilaration, as my brain grappled with what just happened. God had spoken… *to me.*

When the rush wore off and I found myself registered for my first preaching class two months later, God's mandate was little solace. It meant that I was stuck. It also meant that I would have to stand in front of real people and preach for the first time in my life. Yes, God had told me to do it but there was one problem; that meant I would have to *do it.*

You have to know where I was coming from. I was the type of guy who got the jitters in social settings where more than two people could hear me talk. I didn't say much in public and felt painfully shy around those I didn't know. If you put me in front of a microphone, I could feel my chest tighten, the blood would pump to my face, my vision went blurry, and dizziness set in. Not the best credentials for preaching.

So, there I was—less than twenty-four hours 'til the moment of truth. But, I had been preparing. I had studied the power of speech, of all topics, in James 3:1-12. Through the guidance of my good professor, I had learned to apply the basic skills needed to build a sermon from the text. It was flawed, sure, but I had something worth saying. I just wasn't sure I'd have the guts to say it.

Keenly sensing the approach of "zero hour," I mustered up enough courage to speak with my professor. It was hard enough just to spit out a few words to him.

"Uh, Dr. Morris," I began.

"Yes, James. How can I help you?"

"I've never preached before in my life and I'm scheduled to preach in class tomorrow."

He must have understood my unspoken message: "Help!" Dr. Derek Morris is one of the few masters of teaching and he knew just what I needed. "James," he encouraged, "you have written a powerful sermon. Just preach it!"

"Just preach it!" Well, that made sense. I did have something to say. What was I so nervous about? I'd like to say I preached the perfect sermon that day and wowed the class with my skills and brilliance but it was just a beginner's sermon.

Nonetheless, it was a turning point for me. I learned a lesson that has shaped the way I think of preaching in the years since that first sermon: Good preparation makes a world of difference. When you know you have a solid message to preach, you can beat the nerves.

Three Elements In Every Sermon

Six preaching classes and hundreds of sermons later, I've learned a few more tricks for building sermons. Books on preaching have multiplied in recent years as more people realize that the ancient art of preaching can still change the world. For the beginner, this mountain of material is staggering. But, there is good news.

With the dozens of books I've read about preaching and the many lectures I've heard, I am convinced that a simple core runs through it all. Preaching theories are as scattered as the stars but they all owe a debt to the core. If you master the core and lean heavily on God's Spirit, you can master the art of preaching.

Before you get lost in the details, cement in your brain *three* core elements. They are structural ingredients found in every effective sermon. We will explain and expand these elements throughout this book but please catch the concept of each one now.

A life question

Since preaching is the act of helping God's word speak to the life of the listener, the preacher's job is showing how a given part of Scripture speaks to real life. The first element of every sermon, then, is a guiding *life question.* This is a question your listener is already asking. Whether you pose the question outright or just imply it, every good sermon has a guiding question.

Questions might be raised by events or they may be universal question marks that hang in every mind. One example of a guiding question arises from tragedy: "Where is God when bad things happen?" The clarity and relevance of the question you ask the listener will inspire their level of attention.

A biblical answer

The second element of every sermon, then, must be a *biblical answer*. Do you see how this begins to fulfill the purpose of preaching (helping God's word speak to the life of the listener)?

You have begun with a life question. Put another way, you have begun in the listener's world. Now, as you explain the biblical answer, you show how God's word relates to them. You introduce their world to the biblical world.

To the question, "Where is God when bad things happen?" the answer might be, "God is there to comfort the hurting." Your task here is not done until you have answered the life question with biblical truth.

Life application

The third element of every sermon, then, is *life application*. If you miss this step, the listener may go home mentally impressed with truth but it won't change their life. Especially in today's world, where people take *little* time for quiet reflection, you must tell them how the answer can change their life.

Tell them what to do. With the question, "Where is God when bad things happen?" and the answer "God is there to comfort the hurting," the application might be, "When disaster brings pain, pray for God's comfort." Your sermon doesn't succeed or fail *in the pulpit* but later, when your listener faces that life question *in her own world.*

These three elements are the sermon in a nutshell. If your sermon has nothing but these three elements, people *will* listen. And, when these elements are clear in your own mind, your confidence will sore with the knowledge that you have something to say. In time, you won't be a jittering mouse begging for hearers but rather a steady lion that commands attention.

The Spirit of God

And, yet, that's not quite all. However diligent God wants you to be in preparation, never forget that only God can change hearts and only God can give you just the right message. Isaiah understood preaching when he said,

> *"The Spirit of the Sovereign LORD is on me, because the LORD has anointed me to preach good news to the poor. He has sent me to bind up the brokenhearted, to proclaim freedom for the captives*

9

and release from darkness for the prisoners"
(Isaiah 61:1).

God's Spirit will empower you to give the world's questions godly answers. Now for some details....

Development Phase One:

Choose the Anchor Text

Preach God's Word, Not Yours

A sermon is a proclamation of *God's* word. That is serious business. When you stand in the pulpit and deliver a sermon, you are speaking for God. Accepting the invitation to preach is vaguely like stepping up to deliver a speech for the President of the United States. "I'm sorry, the President couldn't be here, so I will share his thoughts with you."

You wouldn't think of passing off your own thoughts as his. When you stand to preach, you are saying, "I'm sorry, God couldn't preach directly, so I will share his thoughts with you."

Scared yet? Good. It's a sobering task. But, don't run. The answer is not avoidance. God calls you to preach. Paul told Timothy, "Preach the Word; be prepared in season and out of season; correct, rebuke and encourage—

with great patience and careful instruction" (2 Timothy 4:2 NIV).

The call is simple—"preach the *Word*," not your own opinions. A common response I hear when I ask people to preach is, "I don't have anything to say." They don't realize that it's best to start that way. The ideas you should convey are *written for you*—Scripture.

Let God Set the Agenda

Your task is to study until you understand it and *then* tell the people how it can change their lives. "For the word of God *is* quick, and powerful, and sharper than any two-edged sword" (Hebrews 4:12 KJV). Can you say the same for your own thoughts? Me neither.

How can you make sure the thoughts you share are truly God's? I recently watched the U.S. president deliver his State of the Union address. A few weeks later, I saw it playing on a friend's computer so I leaned in to watch the familiar speech. But, it wasn't familiar.

It looked the same and the words that matched his lips sounded like his voice but the message was changed. The remixed speech used the president's words, phrases, and even whole paragraphs but it wasn't his message. It was a comic spoof.

Far too many sermons bear this stamp, and usually not by intention. It's easy to string verses together to make your point. But, please don't forget that a sermon should never make *your* point. You are speaking for Someone else.

Learn God's Message in Context

Before you presume to speak for God, you must know what he means to say. If you go to the text with a message in mind, you are in grave danger of passing off your own ideas as God's. If your message is preconceived, it is you who sets the agenda—not God. Approach the text with an open mind.

Resolve that you will never preach until, through careful Bible study, you have learned something new. Be taught by God, and *then* teach others. This hints at a philosophy of approach but, first, a couple of questions....

If you plan to include, say, eight verses in your sermon, which is better—eight verses that *you* place together or eight verses that *God* placed together? And, if you are digging to know the meaning of a text, will the verses around it or verses from somewhere else best explain it? Before you answer, remember the president's speech.

Phase One: Choose the Anchor Text

Because of the human tendency to inject our own ideas into the message, the safest way to prepare a sermon is to let God's word chart the course. That implies a certain approach, which brings us to the first phase in sermon development: *Choose an anchor text.*

By selecting a passage of sufficient length, you can allow God's word to set the direction of your sermon. Your sermon structure, the marks in your line of reasoning, and even some creative aspects can emerge from the text itself. This makes your job easier but it also makes your sermon more biblical. For reference purposes, I call this process *the text led sermon.*

There are three focus questions to help you set the parameters of your anchor text. They help answer the larger question: "How much should I cover?" The twin errors, of course, are choosing too small a text to be sure what it means or too large a text to cover clearly.

In the case of a parable or simple story, the start and end are obvious. But, it is not always so easy to lift a passage from Paul's extended arguments or the collected sayings of Jesus. The three focus questions help clear your thinking about parameters.

A simple point

The first and most essential focus question is, "Can I draw a single, simple point from these verses?" The answer has room for preference. For example, you may choose to draw that simple point from the broad life-story of Joseph or you might choose to draw on a different lesson from just one phase of his story—his resistance to Potiphar's wife or his preparation for famine, perhaps.

Both options are valid. The fundamental issue is whether you can bring the simple point to the surface of the text in a thirty-minute sermon. Your ability to judge this issue improves with practice but your natural instincts will probably bring you close.

A representative portion

The second focus question appeals for integrity: "Do the isolated verses correctly represent the biblical author's thoughts?" Perhaps this is what Paul had in mind when he charged his young protégé, Timothy, "Be diligent to present yourself approved to God, a worker who does not need to be ashamed, rightly dividing the word of truth" (2 Timothy 2:15 NKJV). This Greek word for "dividing" means, "to cut a straight line." It's a picture of meticulous care. No sloppy work.

An example that shows the need for care is Romans 8:31. There we find the rousing words, "If God is for us, who can be against us?" These words have emerged to rouse courage in a soldier's heart or comfort a woman struggling with her boss. Although they warm the heart, these applications have nothing to do with the text.

The idea might seem true and good but that doesn't make it biblical. In fact, the verses that precede these inspiring words show that Paul speaks of God's incredible fight to save us from sin. No sloppy work, please. The truth is more inspiring anyway.

A complete picture

The third focus question asks, "Is any part of the puzzle missing?" This requires that you understand the broader argument that your text is part of. To cite a simple case, in 1 John 2:13, three groups are mentioned—fathers, young men, and little children. Each one represents an aspect of John's message.

It wouldn't be fair to John's message if you preached on only two of these groups and skipped the other. It might be fair to explore just one group and leave the rest for later but, as soon as you pretend to explain his larger argument, which is comprised of three parts, you must include all the pieces.

Another example of the same principle is the parable of the wheat and weeds. Jesus tells the parable early in Matthew 24 but leaves the explanation for later in the chapter. It wouldn't do to preach a sermon on the parable and never study Jesus' own explanation of it.

You could draw creative deductions from its symbols that would impress your audience but they might not be the truth. Make sure no piece of the puzzle is missing, so the picture is as crisp as possible. Remember the president's speech?

Practice: Applying the Focus Questions

This questioning process reminds me of a childhood sleuthing game I played at Christmas time. When mom's back was turned, my brothers and I would inspect the colorful shapes beneath the tree.

First, we checked for size. This usually crossed out a couple of items from our request lists. Then there was weight and the shake-test, which narrowed the options further. And, of course, a quick check for paper-tears or loose seams that might give a peek. Soon, we'd have a fair guess what was in them. It's like this with defining the parameters of your anchor text. Each question brings you closer to that perfect balance between too much and too little.

Let's take a practice text and apply the focus questions. This passage will also serve as a test case for the other phases of sermon development, which appear in later chapters. Using the same text throughout allows you to follow an anchor text through the whole process from text to sermon. For nostalgia, I'll use the text from my first sermon—James 3:1-12.

By citing the verses, you know that I have already settled on the parameters of the text. But, let's step through the process that led to that decision. When we finish here and you understand the process fully, choose a text of your own and apply the focus questions to it.

Be sure to choose a text you want to spend some serious time with, so you can use it as your own test case for each principle you learn. If you are careful to follow each step as you learn it, you will have written your own sermon by the end of this book.

Start by reading the broader section of Scripture that contains your text of interest. By general skills of observation, you will begin to notice the major divisions of thought, like when the subject changes and what is being said about each subject.

Imagine that you are reading the third chapter of James in your morning devotions and you are so impressed with something it said that you have decided to study it more, so you can preach on it. Find a Bible and read it, now, to get familiar with the text. Be sure to read a chapter or two on either side of it, to establish good practice. Focus on the broad flow of the text, without getting lost in the details.

Done? Good. Your initial observation will quickly tell you that the subject of the tongue begins in James 3:1 and ends in verse 12. Before this, in chapter 2, he writes of the relationship between faith and works. And, later in chapter 3, he writes about wisdom from above.

Although it will be helpful to explore the relationship between James' thoughts on the tongue and the subjects surrounding it, that can be left for the next phase of sermon preparation. You know enough from initial observation to set tentative parameters: James 3:1-12. Now you are ready to ply the focus questions to test these tentative parameters.

A simple point

First, "Can I draw a single, simple point from these verses?" To answer this, it helps to reread the selected verses. On second reading, you will start to notice the separate points marshaled in explanation of the larger subject. As the question suggests, you must decide if you can address all that the author says about the subject or just one of his sub-points. In this case, everything he says supports the simple idea that words are powerful. That's preachable.

A representative portion

Second, ask, "Do the isolated verses correctly represent the biblical author's thoughts?" Since we have not chosen one of the sub-points, this question is easier to answer in the affirmative. By contrast, if we chose to speak only from verse 2, about perfection through speech, we might be in danger of building a whole theology of perfection from something that James only meant to illustrate his larger point—that words are powerful. But, since we have taken the entire discourse on speech as our anchor text, we have taken the safe route.

A complete picture

Third, ask the clean-up question: "Is any part of the puzzle missing?" This, too, is easier to answer when we've chosen to address the entire discourse. If we chose only verse 6, that the tongue is set on fire by hell, we might be compelled to conclude that good Christians don't speak.

I suppose the idea might inspire someone but it's awful hard to preach a sermon on that without sounding hypocritical. Besides, it's not the biblical message. James does leave us with a little hint of hope at the end. Similarly, if we chose to preach from the rousing words on the power of speech in verses 3-5, we might highlight the potential of words without sounding the proper warnings.

Do It Yourself

Now it's your turn. You have been reading about it long enough already. Take that first step on the path from text to sermon: choose your anchor text. In the following chapters, you will spend plenty of time with this anchor text. But, your task of the moment is simply to choose it. Don't fret too long over the choice. Almost any text can make for a powerful sermon if you determine to make it a text led sermon.

DEVELOPMENT PHASE TWO:

Study the Anchor Text

Be Intentional About Interpretation

"You can't just read the Bible and do what it says."
His words were a bit shocking but he had a point. My
undergraduate Old Testament professor, Dr. Donn
Leatherman, is a master at wordcraft. He knows just how to
frame an idea to make it notable. I have often contemplated
these words.

He meant to show us that we always *interpret*
Scripture. It is true. You read the story of David's adultery
with Bathsheba (2 Samuel 11) and you interpret David's
behavior as bad. If you just read the story and did what it
said, you'd be sleeping with other people's spouses. Yes,
we always interpret—and we should.

Someone might object and point out that the text
itself shows the reprehensible nature of David's choice.
Yes, it does, but later (2 Samuel 12:1-14). If you are

looking at the story for the first time, it takes some extra study to find this judgment—you have to read the next chapter.

The point is that you always *interpret* the Bible, either through the goggles of your own belief system or through the panorama of Scripture itself. If you don't admit that you have an interpretive scheme, it is destined to run in the background and be driven by your own belief system. This leaves you vulnerable to misinterpretation. The goal is intentionality.

Look At All Sides of the Text

I recently read the story of a former POW who temporarily lost his mind. It followed the pattern of a hundred other stories. After years of starvation and torture, he became paranoid. Even after release, he thought the friends that came to see him were just enemy soldiers dressed up to trick him.

His own experience kept him from seeing the facts. It was only after extended exposure to the truth that he began to see it for what it was. It's like that with biblical interpretation. Your past experience with religion, however good, can keep you from seeing certain truths in the text.

Only after extended exposure to the text can you be sure you've seen the truth.

There's good news, though. If you follow a careful checklist, to insure that you collect all the facts, you can make great strides in breaking past preconceived notions and unlock the living world of Scripture. The keys I am about to share come partly from my own thoughts, partly from the work of Hans Finzel[1], and partly from a plethora of others too numerous to mention.

The thought to grasp is that these guidelines seek to remove blinders that keep you from fully seeing the text. We are often told to study our Bibles but rarely told how. I want to tell you how.

Start broad

The first key is to *start broad*. To understand this principle, let us resurrect the presidential speech analogy from the previous chapter. How much will it tell you about the president's speech if you hear just one word of it? Not very much.

If it is an especially loaded word, like "genocide" or "terrorism," you might *guess* a bit of what he said but only

---

[1] See Hans Finzel, *Unlocking the Scriptures* (Wheaton, IL: Victor Books, 1986).

because you have heard him speak on these subjects before. You wouldn't learn anything new.

If you hear a whole sentence from the speech, if it is a key sentence, like, "Yesterday, we invaded Norway," you will learn more. But, not until you hear an entire paragraph, and preferably the whole speech, can you be sure of his real message.

The same is true of Bible study. Even though Scripture is "God-breathed" (2 Timothy 3:16), it is written in the form of human communication (2 Peter 2:21). You should seek to understand it on these terms. At present, that means understanding the whole before trying to explain the parts.

In the case of James 3, you should read the whole book to see how this discourse on speech fits into James' broader message. As you do, keep a notepad handy to record your findings.

Without getting too specific, we can quickly observe that two grand themes of the book meet in chapter 3. First, James argues that faith must show up in your deeds (2:14). Second, he contends that these deeds should include kindness to each other (4:11). It is a message of practical godliness—the good deeds of a Christian must include kind words.

No doubt, there are many other helpful connections between James 3 and the rest of the book but don't confuse yourself with *too broad* a study until you have written two or three sermons. The goal is simply to understand the larger framework of your anchor text enough to be sure you won't distort it.

Collect all the facts

The second key to careful study is to *collect all the facts*. With notepad in hand, begin to read just your anchor text. Read it like a story and see what facts jump off the page. If the text is a story, then it won't be hard to read it like a story—obviously. But, if you have a text like Paul's dissertation on sin in Romans 7:14-25, it might not seem so obvious.

Yet, every text *is* a story, whether or not it is written like one. There is a story behind key words the author chooses and the people he addresses and why he says what he does. Quite often, these "hidden" stories are indirectly told in the text—you just have to dig for them.

As you collect your facts, to uncover the story, begin by listing the characters. Include all the names, of course, but other key players, like the tongue in James 3, are also characters in the drama. List them among the cast, since they play leading roles in the story.

After you have identified all the actors, note what is said about each one. Next, record any other facts you can see, like when the "story" happened and where. Finally, list key words—words that repeat or seem loaded with meaning. As you reflect on these facts, with a little imagination, a drama will begin to play out in your mind. Let your imagination run.

If this kind of study is new to you, it will probably feel something like my first and only ballet. No, I didn't dance in it. I just sat in the audience. The whole affair came about when a friend and I devised a brilliant scheme for wooing our wives.

We told them to dress in their finest for a mystery date on the town. Then, to throw them off track and increase the surprise, we stopped at a cheap fast-food joint for dinner. But, the evening finally carried us to a stately old opera house and *The Nutcracker*.

As a son of the eighties, I had always frowned at the thought of ballets, so I expected to gain nothing more from the excursion than a pleased wife. At first, I didn't understand the art form. The words in the songs seemed pinched, I couldn't follow the dances, and the plot escaped me.

Then, I started to see patterns. After more exposure, its shapes and moods began to rub a crude image on the canvass of my brain. Before long, I was fully engaged and it made sense! It's like that with careful Bible study—your story perception ability grows with exposure to the details.

It's time to practice. Read the practice text (James 3:1-12) and see what facts you find. Put this book down until you are finished....

Now, let's look at some of the facts you may have found. Since the text is a case of direct address, we should list both audience and author as actors in the opening scene. They mostly pop up in pronouns like "my," "you" and "we."

Next, the hypothetical "perfect man" is introduced by "if"—he's blameless in speech. Ships and forests and beasts all dance onto the stage, with fire and poison to boot.

Then, there is the fascinating fig tree that refuses to make different fruit and the spring that is also stubborn about the kind of water it gives. At center stage is the lead actor: your tongue. And, of course, there are the two characters that play in almost every story: God and humanity.

Other facts fill in the set. The reference to "teachers" reminds us that these instructions apply especially to communicators. The word "stumble" carries the image of *accidents*, emphasizing again just how easy it is to slip up in speech. Other words, like "judgment, perfect, boast, iniquity, hell, tame, unruly, bless," and "curse" render similar insights.

But, the word the story hangs on is that main character, the "tongue." The extremity of the other words—especially "perfect" and "hell"—show the *intensity* of a person's struggle with their tongue. The chief characters in this drama are you and your tongue. The plot grows from your intense struggle to tame it.

Outline the text

The third key is to *outline the text.* This is not a place for creativity. It is like looking over the terrain to draw a map. In this case, the map shows how the biblical author gets from his starting-point to his real point. To preserve the stage metaphor, we might also say it is like cataloguing the scenes in a play.

In the best stories, one scene leads to the next and no scene is really expendable to the plot. If you miss a few scenes, you might not get the full force of the story's end.

As you write your sermon, this catalogue of scenes from the text may serve as the framework of your sermon. Whether it does is your choice but the story's end—the point of the text—must always be the point of your sermon. An accurate text outline helps insure this.

An outline of James 3:1-12 might look like this:

Words control people (3:1-2)

> Example: a horse's bit (3:3)
>
> Example: a ship's rudder (3:4)

Words are a destructive force (3:5a)

> Example: a spark in the forest (3:5b-6)
>
> Example: an untamed beast (3:7-8)

Words should carry a consistent message (3:9-10)

> Example: a spring's product (3:11, 12b)
>
> Example: a tree's product (3:12a)

Viewed as a story, there are three broad scenes. The first scene shows the great power of words over the people who speak them. A horse's bit acts the part of words and directs a massive Clydesdale across the screen. Then, a ship's rudder dawns the same costume and steers a tanker through the docks.

The second scene thickens the plot by showing that words are not only powerful but also destructive. A spark from a careless camper falls on some dry twigs and soon the flames are leaping and roaring through the treetops. The spark also acts the part of words. Next, wild beasts—lions, elephants, badgers, and others—take up the act, resisting the tamer's tactics. But, as they fall under his control, they are forced to relinquish the costume because words can't be tamed.

When all is despair and it seems this evil force called words cannot be stopped, the third scene opens with a peaceful, gurgling spring. The audience begins to relax but is keenly aware that the villain still lurks. This spring is the clue to his defeat. Its power lies in the fact that it wears no costume. It is a freshwater spring, so it gives freshwater.

Another figure of similar character collaborates the clue. It is a fig tree that gives only figs. The fog is lifting. The audience has been obsessed with the result of evil, the words themselves, but the key is the source. The spring, the tree—it all makes sense.

If the power of words has any hope of serving the cause of good, their source will make the difference. As long as the speaker is evil, her words will be also. The words are really a neutral power, long used for evil but waiting for a goodhearted master to wield them.

Condense the point

The fourth key is to *condense the point*. Seeing the text as scenes in a story brings it to life. We can grasp its meaning because we have translated it into our language— the language of story, the language of life. But, one task remains. You must put your finger on the point.

You don't fully understand the text until you can pack its message into a single, simple, memorable statement. Haddon W. Robinson, one of the few great preachers of our time, explains this process very simply.[2] According to Robinson's formula, you should ask two questions of the text: First, what is it talking about? Second, what is it saying about it? Memorize these two questions and learn to ask them of every text.

The answer to the first question should be just broad enough to include the whole passage, and no broader. For example, it might be accurate to say that James 3:1-12 is talking about the Christian life but that is not very helpful because it is not specific enough. Likewise, it is true that

---

[2] Haddon W. Robinson, *Biblical Preaching, 2nd edition* (Grand Rapids, MI: Baker, 2001), 41.

James is talking about the tongue's relationship to beasts but that is too specific. Rather, James is talking about the power of words.

The second question naturally follows—what is he saying about the power of words? Again, the answer should be just broad enough to include the whole passage, and no broader. To say that words are powerful enough to change things is too broad. And, the statement, "words are a power for evil" misses *half* the story. The best answer is two-sided: their goodness or badness depends on the source.

Now, we are ready to craft the preaching idea. Start by putting the answers to your questions together. What is it talking about? The power of words. What is it saying about words? Their goodness or badness depends on the source. Put the two together and we have a summary of the text: the power of words for good or evil is determined by their source.

This would make a clear and somewhat compelling statement to repeat in your sermon but you can do better. Make it catchy, memorable, punchy, and make it speak directly to the life of your listener.

How would you say it to someone who is struggling to clean up his mouth? The statement I settled on when I preached this text in my first sermon was, "When your heart is pure, pure words will follow." It is fairly good but feels too long.

The preaching idea must be both clear and memorable because the whole sermon will rally around this one statement, packing its entire message into these few words. Today, I would choose a statement like, "The wise will speak wisely" or "Wash the heart, not the mouth."

Study Until the Text Matters

This work of studying the text and the art of crafting a preaching idea that breaks through to the listener's mind reminds me of one winter stop in Yellowstone National Park. It was Christmas vacation when five of us set out from college in Tennessee toward home in Washington State.

Since one of the guys in our group had never seen Yellowstone, we charted our course through the east side of the park. We hoped to see wildlife in the snow and we weren't disappointed. As our two-car caravan passed a restroom facility, one colossal buffalo lumbered across the road in front of us. Then, he ambled toward the restroom parking lot.

Following at a distance, we turned in, passing the sign with big letters that read "Warning! Buffalo Gorings!"

Three of these giant creatures eyed us from the other side of a small wooden barrier fence. We cautiously piled out of our cars and walked about a hundred feet, which brought us within thirty feet of the beasts. Breathtaking.

Intellectually, we knew that people were sometimes ripped apart on those towering horns or bludgeoned to death by that two-thousand-pound mass but we felt pretty safe. That was until one bull casually stepped across the fence that stood between him and us. Suddenly that lumbering mass seemed relevant. I never ran so fast.

This is what you must do for your listener—remove the fence. Most of the biblical ideas you preach are familiar to them. They have lived with the idea long enough to be unmoved by it. A goal of careful study is to know the text enough to make its truth fresh, packaging it so it breaks past the fence that makes your listener sleep.

There is also the boundary of time that separates the stories of Scripture from today. Bringing its pages to life in your own mind will make it able to live in your sermon. Knowing the story of the text and shaping the punch line breaks the fence down.

Take a pen and paper and find your way to the anchor text you chose in the last chapter. If you don't understand everything yet, don't let that stop you. The process will make more sense as you practice. What you do understand will be enough to let you mine the text and find its treasure. Apply each step discussed above and you will revel in God's word as it comes to life.

DEVELOPMENT PHASE THREE:

Draft a Message Outline

Understand the Structures of Thought

Structures are everywhere, though you rarely notice them. It's like wearing a hat so long you have to concentrate to feel it atop your head. Each sentence you speak is a structure. When you whisper gossip, there is a structure to the way you tell it.

Your favorite sitcom keeps you watching because it is structured well. The biblical text, as we explored already, has a structure. The trick is to notice these structures so you can apply what you already knew, but didn't know you knew, to sermon crafting.

To cite another example, a grasp of structure makes the difference between a joke told well and one that falls flat. You have to allow time for the build up and the punch line must come at just the right moment.

Make a Map for the Mind

Sermons are more complex than jokes, and a good deal more edifying, but a good structure is still half the task. Your sermon can rise or fall on its structure. It is the map for the minds of your hearers. Without it, they'll get lost.

Just a week before I wrote these words, my wife and I were traveling to a pastors' conference across the state of Pennsylvania. We shot north on I-476 from our home near Philadelphia, planning to catch I-80 across to the western side of the state. We were already late to the conference, due to a wedding I performed earlier that day. Then uncertainty set in. We couldn't recall if I-80 met I-476 directly or if we had to take I-78 across and reach I-80 the back way.

Having no map on hand, we convinced ourselves that I-78 was the right choice. But, I was operating in a lower state of consciousness, after the emotional drain of wedding production, and missed the sign. Thirty minutes later, we realized the mistake.

Taking the next exit, we turned south again. Only after backtracking did we find a gas station with a map. It showed, to our horror, that we had turned around just short of I-80—the road we needed. Yes, we got there but more than an hour later than we would have with a map. Preaching good stuff without structure is like giving your audience all the roads they need but no map.

Three Core Elements of Sermon Structure

Although sermons take myriads of shapes, there are structural elements basic to all good sermons. These elements include a guiding *life question*, a *biblical answer*, and *life application.*

Shaping your sermon is the art of bringing the listener's world and the biblical world together. You begin in their world by raising a *life question* that hangs in the air of their world. Then, you strap on the gear and carefully lead them into the biblical world, where the *biblical answer* they need is waiting.

You can lead them because you have discovered the answer and know the trails. But, the answer is not all they need. You must lead them back to their world, answer in hand, and show them how the answer solves the riddle of life—*life application.* This final step is a call to action.

Which element receives the most attention depends on how much your audience *already* knows. For example, some issues are both perplexing *and* mysterious. The listener has a life question but doesn't know what it is. In this case, you might spend most of your sermon raising and defining the question.

At other times, the question is clear but the biblical answer is murky. If so, you should pour yourself into explaining the text. Then, there are the facts that people know but don't live by. These demand a sermon that leans toward life application.

But, be cautious—don't take anything for granted. Since every audience is diverse and people need reminders, develop all three elements in every sermon. Now, let us explore ways to do this.

The life question

The first element of sermon structure is the life question. This question must be clear in your listener's mind before you give her the answer. The question is her reason to listen. It is better not to preach than to preach without it. But, the need for clarity does not *always* mean you should state the question right away.

Envision that question mark as a hook in your hand. Swing not just for the head but also the heart. Usually, the best way to hook the listener's heart is through a story they can feel. If the life question is, "Why do bad things happen?" you might tell of a heart wrenching tragedy from the news. Suddenly, that question mark hooks the heart. Then, the question matters and they crave an answer.

At this point, you might ask, "How can I be sure I'll be able to answer the question?" That's easy. You start with the answer, and *then* find the question. This is where all that work you did in your anchor text begins to pay off. If you like to watch Jeopardy, this will make sense to you.

Alex Trebek says, "The answer is… two pieces of bread with something between" and the contestant responds, "What is a sandwich?" Your study of the text has led you to its message. This is the answer. Now, you need the question. So, the question is chosen by the biblical answer you already have.

Take an example. The message of James 3:1-12 is that the heart of the speaker determines his words. Put directly, it says, "Wash the heart, not the mouth." The question must be one that is answered by this biblical point. So, the life question is, "How can I clean up my words?" or something to the same effect—"How can I stop yelling?" et cetera.

Once the process is clear, it is very simple. Question: How can I clean up my words? Answer: Wash the heart, not the mouth. Through this process, we make the Bible point matter to the hearer.

The biblical answer

So far, we have searched the biblical world for truth, returned to learn which riddle it solves, and are poised to lead others to that truth. This brings us to the second element of sermon structure—the biblical answer.

We have already seen how to find the answer and we have found it—"Wash the heart, not the mouth." The task remaining is twofold: your audience must both hear it clearly and see it as biblical. This means leading them down the same trails you took to find it, minus the rabbit trails.

Show them the facts in the text that best build its point. By this, you lead them to find it themselves. Make it clear that these biblical facts answer the life question. This means two steps. First, repeat the question to keep them searching. Each fact in the text leads closer to the answer but repeating the question after you've laid each piece reminds the listener that the puzzle is incomplete. Second, explain how each piece relates to the question—what it says and what it doesn't. Stay on task and keep your audience with you.

In James 3:1-12, we've chosen to preach on the overarching message: "Wash the heart, not the mouth." It would have been fine to choose a smaller part of the text, like the part about teachers (verse 1) or the part about Satan using words to destroy (verse 6) but we chose, instead, to follow the whole discourse to its end.

If we had chosen to speak about teachers, we might have tried to place ourselves in the shoes of a teacher or discussed all that Scripture says about teachers. If we had chosen to address Satan's use of words, we might have spent a good deal of time on the specific dangers of words in various situations. But, since we are preaching the punch line, we can afford to address these other issues only as far as they move us toward that punch line.

I recently watched a great movie on DVD. It was so good that I did what I rarely do—watch the deleted scenes. What a mess. It was right to delete them. Though creative, they missed the story. If left in, they would weaken the masterpiece. The same is true when you show too many facts from the text—its story gets muddled.

Stick to the plotline. It's like leading a crew of ten-year-olds through a maze of trails. There are lots of trails, all of them good for reaching their ends. But, the more side trails you wander down, the more kids you lose on the way. Sadly, the attention span of a church audience is equal to that of ten-year-olds. Don't risk losing them needlessly.

The life application

The third element of sermon structure is life application. This is where you link the lives of Amram and Jochebed with those of Jeff and Cindy. It is the art of spanning the gap between Scripture and life. In terms of a drama, it is the emotional payoff—the part that *moves* the audience. In terms of adventure, we have found the truth in the biblical world and led others to find it but still must lead them back to their world and show them what it changes.

Often, before this final step, the listener is convinced but unmoved. Take a common plotline, for example. The movie starts with a mystery man up to some murky business. The audience is not sure what to think—is he evil or misunderstood? Then, a revelation of his love for the leading lady raises the stakes. Now, we must know whether to love him or hate him.

After a flurry of questions and revelations, all the players converge to unmask the characters. The man we thought was good takes a dark turn and the one hope lies with our mystery man. Will he save the girl or will all be lost? In a flash of cinematography, we finally see it—he is good.

Is this enough? Can the movie end here? No. We have answered the guiding question of the story (the first two sermon elements, if you will). But, if the story ends with the answer, it ends as a dud. It hasn't changed the girl's peril.

We hold our breath to see his goodness save her. We must watch the rescue. We must savor the closing kiss. A good sermon without application is like a good love story without the kiss. It's like a rescue story that ends before the rescue.

To make application, be specific. If the biblical answer says, "Put kids first," then tell your audience what that means. Give concrete examples, like, "Play with your kids one hour each day" or "Pray with your kids every night" or "Work less overtime."

Since your audience is diverse, visualize the life situations represented. Put yourself in each pair of shoes, even though some won't fit. Offer a practical suggestion for each group—singles, elderly, parents of young kids, parents of estranged kids, the happy, the sad, the committed, the wayward. Give each person a way to respond to the sermon—a step they can take to apply its message. Say something like, "You can apply this truth in one of the following ways…" and give a list of ideas.

In James 3:1-12, the message strongly hints at application but it still leaves the girl un-rescued and the hero un-kissed. "Wash the heart, not the mouth" tells what to do (and what not to do) but doesn't tell how—it is not specific enough. Begin to think of how the message applies to each person differently. The real goal of *this* message is to put people in contact with God so he can wash their hearts. It is a call to deeper spirituality. = *Transformation*.

James has made an explicit diversion from the problem the reader first sees. The reader sees that she can't stop cursing her sister but James says that is not the *real* problem. He hints that the source, the heart, must change before words will—a point Jesus made before him (Matthew 12:34). So, your applications must address the state of the heart.

For the grandmas, who have never uttered a word more colorful than "cripes," the sin might be gossip. For teenage boys, the sin might be bad words. Whatever the case, name the sin (to raise awareness of need) and list ways to let God cleanse the heart. In this case, the classic spiritual disciplines (prayer, Bible study, meditation, etc.) give the best applications.

We might ask each listener to make a card for their Bible that reminds them to pray—pray they will love their sister enough to stop cursing her or pray that God will help them hate dirty jokes. We might ask listeners to spend time with certain Scriptures that speak of heart transformation and give them a list of texts to read. We might ask them to meditate on the spiritual issues that make them speak ill, with pen in hand, so they can bring those issues to God. Almost any idea that is both specific and serves the sermon's message is fair game.

Three Sermon Design Schemes

There you have it. A sermon consists of a life question, a biblical answer, and life application. This three-part structure is all you need to build a clear sermon outline. With this core, instinct will probably bridge the gaps. Nonetheless, a word about structural variations may broaden your creative horizons. Preaching experts have catalogued thousands of structural schemes but this, too, is really quite simple. Three design schemes form the structure of most good sermons.

Presidential soapbox ⸗ Deductive -

I call the first scheme, the *presidential soapbox*. It is named for its straightforward approach. In a president's soapbox speech, there is little question what his point is, from the start. He lays out his argument, complete with conclusion, and spends his speech telling you why he is right.

The virtue of this design scheme is its clarity. You get the point. Its weakness is that curiosity dies. We know what he said so why listen? If you give the biblical answer early in your sermon, you will need other elements to keep people listening. Good stories or compelling applications will do the trick.

Explorer's quest

The second scheme, the *explorer's quest*, does exactly the opposite of the *presidential soapbox*. You keep them guessing 'till the end. In this design scheme, the guiding question takes over. You guide the audience through a string of discoveries that lead them ever closer to that eureka moment when they find the biblical answer.

The entire sermon still builds toward a single, simple point but the listener doesn't know how the pieces fit together until the end. Suspense is the strength of this scheme because it keeps interest. Its weakness is that it takes more work to keep your purpose clear. The audience needs constant reminders of what you are searching for (i.e. what question you seek to answer).

Text led sermon

The third scheme is the *text led sermon*. This is my favorite. You simply pick up the story of the text and tell it. That means, after you document the logical steps, or scenes, of the text, you build your sermon from its outline. Simple. Paint the scenes, add a few illustrations, make practical applications, and you have a sermon.

This is the easiest design scheme to preach without notes. As you preach through the text, it reminds you of illustrations, transitions, and the rest. The down side of this scheme is that the approach of your specific text *may* not fit your audience.

Design Your Sermon to Fit the Task

Don't choose one design scheme and snub the rest. These are tools in the shed. The task decides which tool is best. When a subject is complex, you need the clarity of the *presidential soapbox* scheme.

If your audience is hostile to the message and you need to convince them before they know it, use the *explorer's quest* scheme—it allows them to see the real issues before they sign you off.

And, if the text's structure answers well to these concerns, use it. Once you have used each design, feel free to combine and experiment. For example, an *explorer's quest* may turn *presidential soapbox* half way through.

Practice: Fitting a Design to the Text

The structure of James 3:1-12 is most like an *explorer's quest*. The question of how to tame the tongue dominates the text and the answer comes at the end. Since the point is not complex, there is no reason to depart from the text outline.

Of course, James gives no modern applications but he gets us close. We can follow his development of the life question (How can I clean up my speech?), dig out the hidden answer (Wash the heart), and then get creative with applications. We have a *text led sermon.*

It is your turn again. Look at the outline you made of your practice text. Could you preach it well through the text's own design scheme? If so, look no further. If not, organize its content to fit the scheme that best fits your audience.

Before you move to the next chapter, make certain those three elements are clearly defined—the life question, the biblical answer, and the life application. Also, write your sermon outline clearly, with verse references.

DEVELOPMENT PHASE FOUR:

Choose Illustrations

Turn Ideas into Pictures

Illustrations are pictures in books that *show* what the book *tells*. They add force to its message. In a sermon, they serve the same goal but the medium has changed. Instead of ink and paper, you have words and the listener's mind. You paint mental scenes with words.

In some cases, you will start from scratch. At other times, you can reuse an image already etched in their brain—instead of painting it fresh, your words bring it into focus. This works best with familiar scenes. Either way, *your goal is to turn ideas into pictures.*

Some readers will thrive on this notion. But, if you are not good with description, don't worry. Many stories and pictures are strong enough to *live* without your help. You can also borrow the talent of others, if you give credit.

"A writer for the *Washington Post* describes the event this way…." Or, "C. S. Lewis tells the story of…."

Even so, it is well worth the work to develop your own skills.[3] You may discover a hidden talent or, at least, improve. Whatever you can do to make the story of the text live will increase impact and retention.

Types of Illustrations

Before exploring *how* to paint good illustrations, we should consider the shapes they take. Most illustrations are stories but stories come in many forms. There are stories from your week, childhood stories, news stories, historical stories, celebrity stories, and others.

There is also common experience to draw from. "We all know what it's like to say the wrong thing at the wrong time." Or, "You know that feeling you get when blue lights start flashing in the rear view mirror? That's the feeling I got when I first read this text."

Quotes are another way to illustrate, adding authority or color to your message. Finally, other Scripture texts can clarify and reinforce the message of your anchor text.

---

[3] The best summary I've seen of stylistic elements is offered by Mark Galli and Craig Brian Larson in *Preaching that Connects* (Grand Rapids, MI: Zondervan, 1994), 81-116.

Illustrations Help You Connect

Illustrating is about connecting. The first rule is, link eyes with your audience. That visual link helps them feel part of the sermon, and it helps you. When you are telling a story to real humans, instead of talking to your notes, social instincts kick in to make it natural.

Illustrations are the easiest part of your sermon to remember, making it easier to tell them without notes. If you would forget the illustration without notes, it's a poor one. If you can't remember it, the audience sure won't. And, it won't work, either, if they go to sleep while you talk to your notes.

Four Keys of Storytelling

That is harsh, I know. We shouldn't say such things to a preacher. But, don't fear. Your audience won't sleep if you apply some keys for crafting illustrations that connect. Since most illustrations are stories, we focus, here, on crafting stories. However, keep in mind that all illustration types enhance the *story* of the text, giving these keys universal application.

Cut the static

The first key is to *cut the static*. Fine-tuning a story is like tuning your radio. You have to remove the "noise" that clutters the mind. How? First, write it down. Then, scratch out all the extra words. Be ruthless. Kill every word that slows speech.

Next, scratch out all facts that don't move the storyline, no matter how interesting. In most cases, you will find the story won't suffer. It may lose some of its color but you will see that it moves better—more like a stride and less like an amble.

Make it live

The second key is to *make it live*. Put some color back in the story. Take a mental trip to the place it happened. Stand there and look around until it seems real. Notice the carpet and lampshades or mud floors and oil lamps. Only when you *experience* the story can you create that experience for others.

By cutting the static, you have stripped the story to its bones. Now, put some flesh back on it but don't put back the static. Add only what keeps the story at a stride. Build its muscle but don't make it fat. Anything that slows it down hinders the story and its power to illustrate.

One way to keep it moving is choosing colorful verbs and nouns instead of adjectives and adverbs. Take an example: "The little bird flew quickly past the window." There is nothing wrong with the sentence but it lags. Say it aloud. It doesn't roll off the tongue right, does it? We can do better.

Cutting the adjective, "little," and the adverb, "quickly," speeds it up. We get, "The bird flew past the window." Try the tongue test again. Smoother? Yes, but we lose some color. This is where colorful verbs and nouns can help. Replace "bird" with "finch" and "flew" with "shot" and you get, "The finch shot past the window." Much better.

Sharpen it

The third key is to *sharpen it*. Identify the point of comparison between the idea you wish to illustrate and the illustration. Then, cut the facts that distract from it. It is okay if the story changes, as long as you are still telling the truth.

Stories are only a snapshot of real life. By changing the story, you are just cropping the shot. To preserve the story of the *text*, you may have to sacrifice some elements of the *illustrating* stories. That's okay. Illuminating the text is what counts.

Aim for the heart

The fourth key is to *aim for the heart*. Illustrations float best in a pool of tears—whether happy or sad. If facts were enough, you would need *few* illustrations. It is true that *some* illustrations clarify but most add heart to the sermon.

Even macho men run on emotion. It might not be sappy emotion but a rousing call to heroics or duty or indignation is also emotional. People decide with their hearts. We could debate the merits of this fact but it remains fact. Your sermon is powerless without a heart appeal. This was true even for Christ's apostles (Acts 2:37).

The Four Keys Applied

Let me "illustrate" each of these four keys with an old story. The story of Abraham Lincoln is complex but always told simply. Questions still swirl about his motives for the War Between the States; he made tactical blunders when the war did commence; but his story is told *without this static* so the true strength of his vision can emerge.

The best tellers of Lincoln's story are Civil War historians and battlefield curators because they have "lived" in Lincoln's world enough to *make him live* in ours, complete with hat and boots. The years of telling and retelling his story have *sharpened it to such a point* that every student knows his imprint on America.

But, the reason for telling it is that *it stirs the heart*—to duty, to sacrifice, to love for something bigger than self. Well-told stories shape the world.

Illustrate with Purpose

But, story is not enough. In fact, "good illustrations" do *not* exist alone. They are only "good" if they illustrate your text well.

I recently found the story of a young mother who suddenly went blind. For twenty-six years, she suffered. She missed the change in each child's maturing face. She never *saw* her grandchildren. Such tragedy. Then came more tragedy.

Medics rushed her to the hospital with a heart attack. Her organs were failing. She was lifeless. But, after hours of work, the doctors (or, God) brought her back. And, wonder of wonders, after twenty-six years, her sight was back too—a medical miracle! When I read it, you can bet I wanted this story for a sermon but I had to be cautious.

A story this powerful can actually destroy the sermon, if misapplied. It's dynamite but you don't want dynamite in the wrong place. If we wish to illustrate the point of James 3:1-12, "Wash the heart, not the mouth," this story will hurt the sermon.

Everyone will retain the story but miss the point of the text. A story about someone who overcame cursing through prayer may not be as dramatic but serves the sermon much better. Save the woman's story in a file until you find its fit.

It wasn't long before I found a place to use it. I was preparing to explain the book of Habakkuk to high school students when something clicked. In his book, Habakkuk asks two questions. Seeing how the innocent suffer at the hands of evil men, Habakkuk cries out to God, "Why do you tolerate wrong?" (Habakkuk 1:3). This is the same question that blind woman must have asked for twenty-six years—why do I suffer and God does nothing?

God answers Habakkuk with a promise to send Babylonian armies and punish Israel (1:6). That gives rise to a second question—how can God use *worse* people to correct Israel? (1:13). It's not fair. But, God doesn't answer the fairness question. He just says it will work out (2:1-20). The book ends with Habakkuk's confession of faith. In essence, he says, "It doesn't make sense but I trust you" (3:17-18). The blind woman certainly would not have asked for a heart attack—it wouldn't make sense—but it gave back her sight after 26 years. The woman's story strengthens the point that, though life seems unfair, God is trustworthy. That's Habakkuk in a nutshell.

Match Strength to Strength

Your strongest illustration should reinforce your main point. Listeners remember good stories. Make sure the one they remember *best* is the one that drives home your *main* point—either the *biblical answer* or *life application.*

This does not mean you will only tell one story or use one illustration for each sermon. Just make the others less fantastic. They should be short and just enough to tack down one scene in the text before moving to the next. Make the force and length of each illustration equal to the weight of the point it serves.

When to Illustrate

By this time, you have enough information to build good illustrations. Now it's time you think of *where* to use them. Every good sermon starts in the listener's world, making a true-life story one of the best ways to raise the life question.

One creative option is that, with just the right story, you can tell it in two parts. To introduce the sermon, tell the perplexing part, the part that sparks the question. Then, when you have shared the biblical answer, tell the part that shows how this truth helped the main character. Or, use two separate stories to serve the same goals.

Use your strongest illustration for your sermon's conclusion and the second strongest for the introduction (except, or course, with a two-part story). The introduction is where you prove your sermon worth hearing and your conclusion is where you drive in its point. For both, you must capture the heart.

Other types of illustrations, like factoids, anecdotes, comparisons, statistics, and the like, may also capture the heart. But, most of these have less impact and work best for illustrating scenes in the text flow. Don't illustrate points smaller than the major scenes, or sermon movements. A good sermon will have at least one and no more than six illustrations.

In summary, there are three spots for illustrations: to introduce the life question, to encapsulate the building blocks that lead to the biblical answer, and to drive the main point through the heart.

Avoid Leaky Illustrations

The most important rule to remember is that illustrations are a communication device, a medium, through which we *funnel* a message. Their ability to funnel the message is their one test of value.

When we were children, my two brothers and I communicated secret messages with cans and string. The tension in the string carried the vibrations of our voices from one can to the other.

Later on, we thought we had improved our covert communications mechanism by speaking into the heater vents at opposite ends of the house. The heating ducts carried our messages too, without the bother of wind or broken strings.

There was one problem. As we sent our covert, after "bedtime," messages from one end of the house to the other, our words escaped to the vents in other rooms—the ones with parents in them. So much for stealth. . .

Although cans with string is a lesser device than heater vents, the vents allowed our message to leak out and defeated the purpose. Remember the lesson of the heater vents when choosing your illustrations. Don't look for the best story but the best illustration of the biblical point. Avoid leaky communication media.

Practice: Illustrating James 3:1-12

Let us illustrate James 3:1-12. This text carries its own illustrations, in the form of metaphors (ships, fire, et cetera). They encapsulate the scenes of the story but they are far from the listener's world. Although understandable in today's world, most listeners don't live with ships or forest fires. We can use them for clarity but we must *start and end* in the listener's world with stories *close* to their heart.

The life question is, "How can I clean up my words?" The best illustration to raise this question is the most direct. Find a story about someone who struggled to stop cursing others. Better yet, tell on yourself. No doubt you have stumbled in speech.

The biblical answer is, "Cleanse the heart, not the mouth." The best illustration for this concept is a story of someone's changed heart that changed their speech. If you can't dig up a story that direct, find one that shows how a changed heart kicked another habit. The real point is that you can't change yourself; God must change your heart. If you illustrate this concept, you can explain how it applies to speech.

How to Find Illustrations

We have learned why, how, and where to use illustrations. One task remains—finding illustrations—a task that intimidates every budding preacher. There's good news: illustrations are everywhere. Having good illustrations comes from *seeing* them more than *finding* them.

Look for them in life

You can learn to see illustrations with a simple practice. Carry a palm-sized notepad, index cards, or a small recorder. Whenever something interesting happens to you, think of what it illustrates and record it. Do the same with interesting news stories, quotes, movie scenes, memories, or whatever you experience in life.

My best illustrations come from childhood memories or the news. It might seem hard at first but you will soon have more illustrations than you can use. Organize them into file-folders on your computer (or the old fashioned way), so you have them when you need them.

Look for them in Scripture

Illustrating your text with other Bible texts is more complex. It is still wise to keep track of insights you find through personal study, like you would daily experiences, but there is more.

First, only use illustrating texts that you have studied. Misused texts weaken your message. Second, don't use more than six illustrating texts. Too many will splinter the sermon's punch. You can find the right texts with a concordance, through cross-references in your Bible, or with software.

Practice: Spend Time Looking

Spend the next two days collecting illustrations from life and Scripture, and then take the sermon outline you made and see what fits. You might be surprised how much does fit. If there is nothing, read the news or review your childhood memories. Something good will surface. As a last resort, read a book of collected stories. The right illustrations are close by. With time, you will learn to see them.

DEVELOPMENT PHASE FIVE:

Write Useable Notes

Useable Notes Help You Remember

The mind has a way of forgetting things when you need them and recalling things at just the wrong moments—like forgetting your sermon flow and remembering that you're scared of public speaking just when you step on stage. There is hope. It has much to do with prayer and something to do with writing useable notes. Since you likely know something about prayer, let's address the issue of notes.

The term "useable notes" does not mean you will have them *in the pulpit*. It means organizing your thoughts for recall, so you have them *in your head*. Useable notes make it easier to internalize and recall your sermon. Ideally, you will depend on them to prepare but not to preach. They must be concise, so there's less to memorize, and hit just the big stuff—the main points.

Useable Notes Help You Preach Note Free

You can practice the art of seeing the big stuff next time you watch a movie or story-based program. As you watch, jot down the major movements of the story. With just the list you make, you can repeat what matters to the storyline, either in detail or in summary. Try it. It works. With the same tact, you can preach your sermon—*without notes*. That is how useable notes work.

Preaching note free is easy

Preaching without notes takes method, not genius. Prepare your sermon like scenes in a play. Then, you need only recall the order of scenes. The details of each scene will come to mind with that scene.

Your notes just trigger the scenes in sequence. Memorizing this sequence will allow you to memorize very little and preach note free. If you forget a few trifles, it won't hurt the story. And, you will gain poise and audience connection.

Preaching note free is better

Too often I have laid a thick manuscript on the pulpit, only to lose my place and render it useless. Most times, that was a good thing. Time and again, I learn the same lesson: When you know your core message and the basic steps needed to get there, you *can* preach without notes.

Dozens of times, I have stepped on stage with a jittery sermon on paper and left with a spiritual powerhouse that came from the heart. A manuscript in the pulpit feels like a security blanket but does more harm than good. There is a better plan.

The Process of Note Development

That plan starts with the security blanket—write the manuscript. Make it a full transcript of the message—every word. This helps you think through it. Write careful transitions between scenes, that review the last one and preview the next; write an introduction that grabs attention and lays out the guiding question; craft crisp language that moves; and draft a conclusion that reviews the sermon and drives home its message. Writing a manuscript *develops* the sermon and *preserves* it for years to come.

Start with a structure

Let's start at the beginning. Useable notes demand structure. The message outline from phase three of sermon preparation is a great start. This is the sermon blueprint and should govern every step of its construction.

The structure of your sermon holds it up and is enough to show what the rest will look like. Writing it means filling in these details and remembering it requires knowing the structure. If you know the structure, you can recall where the details go. But, of course, the details must be chosen first.

Add illustrations

The illustrations developed in phase four have begun to add drywall and lighting but you can't show the house just yet. If you have ever watched a house being built, you know that its framing shows enough to see where the rooms are and how big they are. But, no one enjoys the house until the details are done.

Add transitions

The first details to hang on the structure, after the illustrations (drywall and lights), are transitions. These are the doors from one room to the next. Write transitions that review and preview. For example, "So far, James says that words cause damage. What he says next is more hopeful."

Just like a door, one side should connect with one scene and the other with the next. A brief look back at where we've been, followed by a nod in the direction we're going, keeps the audience with us. Good transitions help both preacher and audience see and remember the connection between scenes.

Write a gripping introduction

Next, write an introduction that grabs attention and lays out the guiding question. Starting the second you step to the pulpit, you have thirty seconds to clinch interest. If you fail then, it's tough to win it later. In construction terms, the introduction is curb appeal.

I've seen some spectacular sermons that nobody listened to because they started slow. A fast-paced story, a stunning statistic, a shocking or intriguing question or statement—any of these can do the trick. It should feel natural and energetic. If the introduction is too much work for the preacher to spit out, it is too hard for the audience to listen.

Your introduction must do two things: get attention and introduce the guiding, life question. Put another way, introduce the subject and make it matter to the listener.

Add colorful language

So far, you have a structure, you have an introduction, and you have transitions between points/scenes. But, the house still needs paint—paint each scene in clear and compelling colors. By "paint," I mean, explain the points of the text with memorable language.

Next to clarity, it's most important to craft language that *moves*. Sermon language, even more than written language, must be simple. Give it the tongue test. Does it roll off well or get slowed down with awkward syllables and extra words? Write short, punchy, simple sentences. "James means to tell us that we should carefully consider the ramifications of the words we choose" is not near as good as, "Choose words well."

Add style

Even so, "extra" words *can* serve a purpose. But, only use them if that purpose is clear. For instance, "Choose words well; select with care; make sure they come from God," says little more than "Choose words well" but it adds force. Like illustrations, put your best tools behind your big points.

Remember, dynamite in the wrong place is destructive. Use such techniques sparingly, strategically. A number of books have been written on stylistic elements but the best way to learn these is by hearing them. Listen to recordings of your favorite preachers and note the techniques that work. You will, over time, develop a sense for when "extra" words help. Until then, simplify, simplify, simplify.

Write a compelling conclusion

Just one step remains to finish your first draft: write a concise, compelling conclusion. Draw all the weight of your sermon's parts together, causing the listener to feel the full force of your message in a single stroke. This is the finish work on your house that makes the rest inviting.

Review the sermon's logical steps, or scenes, and then drive in its message. Driving that nail home takes four hammer blows: Allude to previous illustrations, repeat your summary sentence, make *specific* applications, and add one last story for the heart.

First, allude to previous illustrations. As you preach, your experience is much different than that of your audience. *You* are concerned with remembering all your points. *They* casually listen for random tidbits. *You* have entrenched yourself in the message of the text and lived its pathos. *They* hear it for the first time, with just your summary. *You* see the points first and the stories second. *They* remember the stories.

Those stories are your most powerful tools. Don't set them aside when it counts most. Emotions have peaked with the punch line of each story. If you stack those peaks under your final message push, it will find its place in their heart.

Second, repeat your summary sentence. This is the message in concentrate form. It is what rides on those emotional peaks. Repetition aids memory and draws attention to the point. A great technique is the story-point-story-point... pattern. Repeat the emotional peak of each story, and then lay down that summary sentence. Keep up the rhythm until all those peaks are spent.

Take an example. (Story allusion:) "When all seemed lost, Charlie found a friend. (Summary sentence:) God is near. When Sarah knelt at gunpoint, praying for a miracle, she got one. God is near. When Elijah ran to Mount Horeb in search of God, he learned that God had been there all along. God is near."

Third, make specific applications to real life. Since you have already identified the various life situations of your audience and made applications (see phase three), the present task is clarity. First, acknowledge diversity. "This message applies in various ways." This signals the audience to look for applications specific to them. Second, state the options in "If...then" form. "If you are lonely, [then] say aloud, 'God is near.' If you are scared, [then] open God's word and read the great stories of his nearness." Give them something to take home and do.

Fourth, add one last story for the heart (see phase four). Your sermon may or may not need this touch. If the story-point-story-point... pattern has done the trick, leave it alone. But, if your arsenal of illustrations is small, add one that encapsulates the point. Keep it short and clear. If it needs explained, don't use it. The story should speak your point so well you don't *need* to say it.

Remember, it's not about looking creative, displaying your genius, or the chance to tell a good story; it's about driving a message from the Almighty through your listener's heart.

Re-outline the Sermon

You now have a manuscript. Take a deep breath and smile. Most sermons don't get this far. But, even with a manuscript, you're a few steps away from usable notes. Next, take that manuscript and graph it. The outline might have changed in the sermon-writing process, so re-outline it.

List its scenes—just a brief sentence of each. It won't take long. You may feel the need to scribble a few scene details under each heading, such as text references and illustration reminders. That is okay. Just be sure to distinguish between the heading and the details (by indenting the details on your notes) so you can see the sequence of scenes at a glance.

Add to this sequence of scenes your written transitions, your introductory paragraph, and your concluding paragraph. You will memorize these elements. Useable notes include all that you must memorize because that it what you should *use* them for.

Even if you take them into the pulpit, their simplicity will leave you free to preach without fear of forgetting or that nasty note reading. They are not the house but rather the blueprint—everything you need for reconstructing the house.

You may have noticed that we switched metaphors, in this chapter, from travel to building. "Blueprint" offers good imagery. But, if you prefer, it is a *map* for leading the audience from their world to the biblical world and back again.

It doesn't show you every tree or hill or stone but it provides enough to know where to go next when you're there. That is all you need. More information may confuse you.

Hard Work Will Pay Off

There you have it. The process of making useable notes is hard work but it is key to lifting the ceiling on your preaching. If you strive to soar above mediocre, the work will pay off. And, there is more good news: it gets easier with practice. For preachers who do it consistently, it is almost second nature. Finally, God helps those who resolve to serve him with excellence.

Grasping After Fluency

Immerse Yourself in Your Notes

Six months is a short time to learn a language but three weeks is more effective. The difference? Immersion.

To prepare for our trip to Germany, my wife and I spent six months learning German from books, CDs, software, and even sermons we downloaded from Internet.

It helped. We became about 30% effective at conversing in German by the time we left for Germany. Our trip was only three weeks long but, by the end of it, we were more like 70% effective. Immersion made the difference.

Preparing to preach is like learning German. For both, the goal is fluency. The difference is that speaking German requires you to be fluent in a language while preaching takes being fluent in your sermon material. Both come best by immersion.

But, don't let this talk of language learning scare you. Preaching is much easier. Your notes are not a *foreign* language at all. You wrote them.

Memorizing Your Notes

We call them "useable notes" for a reason. Now, let's explore how to *use* them. In a phrase, "memorize them." Before you think you can't, try it. You may know them already. Close your eyes and see how much you can recall. More than you thought, eh? It can be done, and without much work—especially since this material is not new to you. Internalizing your notes takes four easy steps.

Learn the scene sequence

First, memorize the scene summaries until you can say them without trouble. We have explored this story-sermon concept in depth. If the sermon is formed into cohesive scenes, you need only a mental kick to trigger the scene and the details will come.

This works when the kick is a short sentence on paper. But, if it *is* short, there is not much to remember. Why not etch the scene list on your brain? That way, you have no paper to lose your place on. It could make life easier.

If you're a visual learner, keep the list in your mind's *eye*. Fix an image of the page in your brain or a picture of the list carved on granite or written in the sky. Whatever works—the goofier, the better. If you are auditory, say them aloud, with gusto, until you can hear yourself saying them even when you're not. It might help to say them with rhythm or sing them.

If you go by feel (kinesthetic), attach each scene to one finger and touch that finger to your thumb when you repeat the scene summary. Following the same action when you preach will help you recall it. Be creative and use a combination of memory aids. I call them *recall devices*.

Learn transitions

Second, using the same recall devices, memorize transitions. These should be easier than the scene list because transitions are simply a review of the last scene and a preview of the next. So, if you know the scene list, you basically know each transition.

The task remaining is just to get crisp language fixed in your mind. Spend less time on transitions. Repeat each one several times. Then, practice everything together—mentally go through the list of scenes, adding transitions. After a few runs through, it should feel comfortable. This is all you need. Relax. The language will come to mind when you need it.

Learn key language

Third, memorize other key language—phrases or clever sayings you want to recall. Don't try too hard on this one either. Repeat the phrases five to eight times and then let them flow naturally. Don't force them.

If they aid communication at the time you present, they will come to mind easily. If you don't recall them, you probably don't need them. Trying hard to memorize every word you've written will damage your presentation, not help it. Tuck favored language into your mind and let come what may.

Learn the introduction and conclusion

Fourth, memorize the introduction and conclusion. Your first words win or lose interest. Your last words secure the message. You can't afford to ramble or seem lost at either place. Memorize at least the first three sentences and the last three of your sermon.

The first two minutes are also your most nervous. Having three sentences to say with punch and confidence will get you past the jitters. In your last thirty seconds, you must drive the message home with force. Keeping language tight adds momentum.

Allow Germination Time

Once you have ingested your sermon, stop. Don't practice for a while—maybe a whole day. It needs germination time. After a little practice, time away from your notes gains more than continued practice.

For most people, it works best to sleep on it. The next best thing is to take a walk, play a game, or read a book. Your mind will work on the sermon subconsciously and, when you come back to it, you'll be miles ahead. You will find that you remember most of it and just have a few details left to sharpen. This means, of course, you must finish writing sooner than the night before you preach.

Strategically Reduce Stress

Most energy spent preparing is wasted. It's like the dog that wears himself out trying to break his chain, leaving no energy for play when his master unchains him. Fear of failure takes more work to beat than learning your sermon. So, know yourself. Notice what lessens anxiety.

Start early

The first anxiety buster is starting early. Remove those chains of fear that waste energy before you've strained at them all week. The earlier you start, the less anxiety you'll suffer.

Anxiety militates against both creativity and your ability to memorize. I find that reading my notes just before I crawl in bed works best. I always wake up knowing them. Maybe it's because it's hard to feel anxious while I'm sleeping.

Seek God's Spirit

The best anxiety buster is the Almighty Spirit of God. His presence is calming and empowering. You cannot change your audience for eternity. Without God's Spirit, you are, at best, an entertainer. But, with him, you *cannot* fail. Pray for his presence as you study, as you prepare, as you preach.

The absolute necessity of God's Spirit reminds me of a story. It was my first shot at long-distance dating. It was also my last one, since I married the girl four years later. After a summer together, this beauty went her way (college in Texas) and I went mine (college in Tennessee). But, I was still captivated. It was a thirteen-hour drive between her college and mine but I drove it. One of us made the trek almost every other weekend.

On one such occasion, I borrowed my brother's car and enlisted a crew of companions to share costs and driving time. All went well until we hit Minden, Louisiana around 3am. I was asleep in the passenger's seat when a growing awareness of something wrong pulled me awake.

The engine was clattering. I asked the driver how long it had been making that sound. My brain began the same unsettled clatter when I heard his response; "About half an hour." I said, "Pull over." Just then, whatever was clattering got tired of it and escaped through the side of the engine block, making its own way out.

We were stuck in a strange town at 3am. It was 591 miles from home and 256 miles from my girlfriend. After an early morning bus ride, a friend's borrowed truck, and a last-minute rescue effort by my brother and his girlfriend, we were saved. That was good but how much nicer to just have an engine.

The tow truck driver remarked on how nice the car looked. I'm sure he meant well but it didn't do us much good without an engine. Do you see the parallel? Your sermon can be a literary masterpiece and not change lives.

The Holy Spirit is the driving force behind all effective preaching. It's the engine... and so much more.

> *"The Spirit of the Sovereign LORD is on me,*
> *because the LORD has anointed me to preach good*
> *news to the poor. He has sent me to bind up the*
> *brokenhearted, to proclaim freedom for the captives*
> *and release from darkness for the prisoners..."*
> (Isaiah 61:1 NIV).

That is *your* commission. It is the task this book has laid before you. Fulfill it as one "who does not need to be ashamed and who correctly handles the word of truth" (2 Timothy 2:15 NIV).

Appendix 1

Sermon Checklist

A sermon starts by picking a fight with a problem and the whole process of preaching it is using your moves to beat it. It's time to review your moves. We now shift from formulation to quality management. If you can spare the time, let a day or two lapse between stages. This freshens your eyes to see flaws. Regardless of time elapsed, however, a good checklist can help you edit *somewhat* objectively. In time, you will add to this list but what follows is basic.

Every good sermon has key ingredients. In some ways, it's like making cookies. Though cookies are as varied as the flowers in a field, most cookies require basic elements—flour, sugar, shortening, water, eggs, and salt. Every sermon has its basic elements, too—life question, biblical answer, life application, illustrations, and a summary statement. Keeping these ingredients well measured is the task of the checklist. We'll limit our checklist to seven diagnostic questions.

1. Is the guiding question clear? The clarity of our life question directly affects the sermon's *sense* of purpose. It sets out the sermon's goal, directing all that follows. Its presence should be felt at all times so the listener knows how each part of the sermon relates to its purpose (answering the question). Repeating some form of the question at key times is the best way to keep clarity.

2. Does the sermon avoid tangents? Don't let the negative term "tangent" throw you off. It doesn't mean bad thoughts or false ideas—just stuff that doesn't help pose or answer the guiding question. No matter how good your ideas may be, if they don't help answer the life question, they'll weary your audience and dilute your message. Be ruthless. Cross them out. Save them for a sermon they fit.

3. Is the use of illustrations effective? The key word is, "emotion." Next to it is, "clarity." Third is, "momentum." These are the prime tests of an illustration's impact. If it fails to add emotional force, you will do best to skip it. Besides emotional force, each illustration should speak to the text and keep up the pace. Remember the acid test: Does it advance story of the text?

4. Is the guiding question answered clearly? It's not enough to say it. Have you made it so clear and prominent that everyone knows the answer? Clarity depends on the right level of analysis. Do just enough text explanation to be clear and stop before you lose anyone in the details. Beyond this, repeat, repeat, repeat.

5. Is the answer convincingly biblical? The audience should walk away with a list of reasons why your answer to life's question is biblical. Periodically stopping to repeat these reasons helps. Make them concise. Your sermon's *biblical* strength is an element that you must never compromise. If your illustrations are poor, you'll do better next time. If your sermon is slow, better next time. But, if your sermon is unbiblical, you have no right to preach.

6. Is the message made practical? In other words, does it change my life? Almost any message can change minds but it takes extra finesse to change actions. You can't make anyone walk the biblical road but you can make clear what the next step looks like. Remember to give them concrete things to do in response to your message.

7. Does the whole sermon feel natural? Those intangible elements that you just know but can't quite explain do matter. And, with closer analysis, they are usually explainable. It often means one of the core elements (question, answer, or application) needs sharpening.

If you can answer these seven diagnostic questions in the affirmative, your sermon is ready to preach. Preach with confidence. You have something to say!

Appendix 2

The following sermon development worksheet offers a step-by-step guide to the process described in this book. You have permission to make as many copies of it as needed for your personal use.

Sermon Development Guide

- Choose an anchor text (day one)

- Study the anchor text (day two)
    - Identify what the text is talking about (the specific subject)

    - Identify what the text is saying about its subject (the specific message)

    - Formulate a punchy, short, memorable, catchy sentence, that summarizes the text's message, to be used in your sermon

- Create a message outline (day three)
    - Choose your guiding question based on the point your biblical text makes

    - Choose the steps you will use to guide your audience through an answer search process

- o Choose what specific practical applications you will make

- Choose the specific illustrations you will use (day four)
    - o Choose an illustration that raises the guiding question

    - o Choose illustrations to help in the answer-search process

    - o Choose your strongest illustration to enforce your summary sentence

- Write out the sermon word for word (day four)
    - o Begin with the outline you developed over days three and four (above)
    - o Fill in each part of your outline with the purpose of leading to the next part of your outline (this will help you stay focused)
- Practice and polish the sermon (day five)
    - o Read it out loud with a pen in your hand to correct and refine awkward language, unclear parts, or poor transitions
    - o Memorize the outline, the transitions, the introduction, and the conclusion

Appendix 3

Developing your preaching skills requires occasional evaluation. The following evaluation sheet is designed to help. You can use it in one of two ways: give it to others or use it yourself. Listening to or watching a recording of your sermon allows you to evaluate yourself. You have permission to make as many copies of this sheet as needed for your personal use.

Sermon Evaluation Sheet

Was the guiding "question" clear?
1   2   3   4   5   6   7   8   9   10

Did the preacher avoid tangents?
1   2   3   4   5   6   7   8   9   10

Was the use of illustrations effective?
1   2   3   4   5   6   7   8   9   10

Was the "question" answered clearly?
1   2   3   4   5   6   7   8   9   10

Was the "answer" clearly biblical?
1   2   3   4   5   6   7   8   9   10

Was the instruction practical?
1   2   3   4   5   6   7   8   9   10

Did a summary statement emerge?
1   2   3   4   5   6   7   8   9   10

Was note use without distraction?
1   2   3   4   5   6   7   8   9   10

Was body language effective?
1   2   3   4   5   6   7   8   9   10

What is your overall impression?
1   2   3   4   5   6   7   8   9   10

Total out of 100: _____

CPSIA information can be obtained at www.ICGtesting.com
Printed in the USA
BVOW011349150812

297970BV00001B/7/A